Oceans of Love

Part 2 of 3

Bhavesh Ramji

*** OM SHANTI ***

Oceans of Love: Part 2
Copyright © 2022 Bhavesh Ramji
Cover Illustration & Interior Art by Bhavesh Ramji
Cover Design by Soulful Group

We unlace words & detangle life
@soulfulgroup | www.soulfulgroup.com

ISBN: 978-1-8381149-5-4

CONTENTS

*** OM SHANTI ***

CONTENTS

*** Om Shanti ***

Oceans of Love: Part 2 is a collection of poems and reflections that takes the reader on a journey of *Awakening to Divinity*.

Whichever way we choose to see Divinity - as a Divine being, as God or as the Cosmic Benevolent Force of the universe, the truth is that the Divine has been the bedrock of many religions and cultures for thousands of years. The Divine has been referenced and honoured throughout history and these time-old questions have fascinated me:

- What is our relationship with Divinity?

- Can we make this relationship close and personal?

- Do we need to follow any rituals or customs of religion to connect to the Divine?

I was inspired to write this collection of poems to help answer these questions for myself and now I am sharing them with you.

I thank you for taking time to read this book and I value your contribution to my journey which is far from complete.

Bhavesh Ramji – Poet, Yogi, Artist

The Incarnation

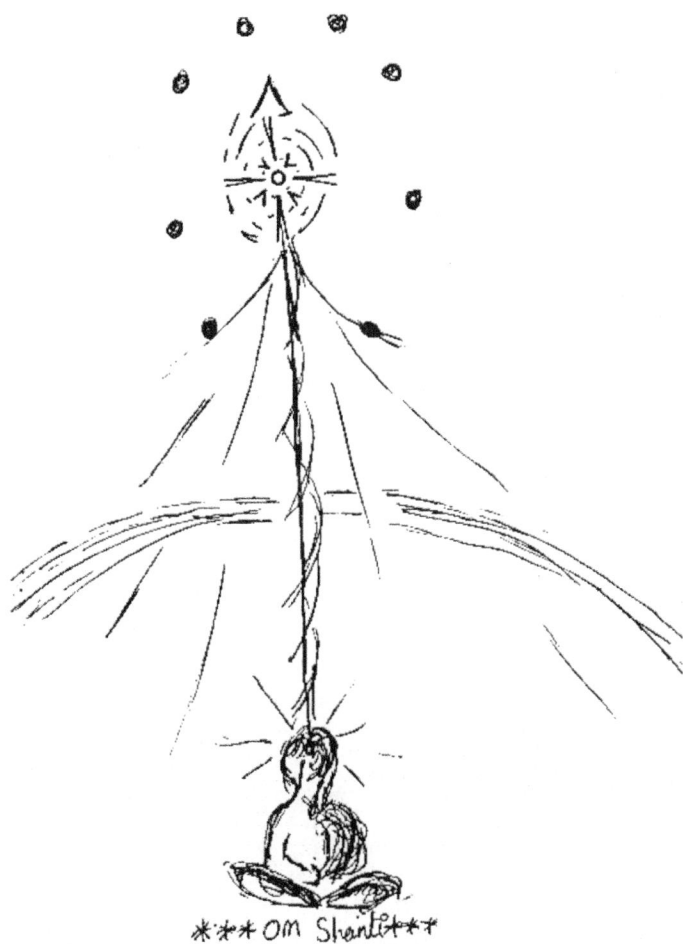

*** OM Shanti ***

Awakening Of Divinity
*** Om Shanti ***

This poem is a memorial of the moment Divinity becomes alive in our lives, where we start to drop the egos of human conditioning and when we become *soul aware*.

At this moment, we start our relationship with Divinity and see his/her creation (the material world), with appreciation and detachment.

The quality of our thinking, words and actions change with this soul awareness as there is inner peace and a loving attitude towards ourselves and others.

This poem gives advice on how we can become *spiritually intelligent.*

Incarnation, the beginnings of creation
Takes a unique birth, on this earth
Comes in the night brings peace to the fight
Removal of tension, beginnings of ascension
A moment so true, new
From the edge of a knife
Breathes new life
Intoxication within cast, so vast
No ocean can fill, so high, no sky can sill
Changes the poses, into spiritual roses fully blooming
If ego comes, it tilts, the roses begin to wilt
You put to one side, relationships gap now wide
Now to be free of this suck
That covers you in muck, put on this tilak*
One of purity in thoughts, words and deeds
The mind is a silent light, fills with gentle might
Free from the earth and increases its worth
You will become capable, your stage unshakable
Words of this creation, love and purity, the vibration
Deeds, just let it be, for all to see
Actions of a karma yogi**
So, continue to check the chart, am I a true art ?
Purity is the path, remain courageous and fearless
To be merged in love, to keep the intellect clear
Remove the fears and listen with your ears
Enjoy this drama and all its varieties of karmas
Cheerful and full, watch for any subtle pulls
The ones of praise, ego raises
The ones of defamation, a difference in nations (opinions)
Remain on your feet, through victory and defeat
A stage of total equanimity

* Tilak – in Indian culture this is the dot placed in the centre of the
forehead, symbolising the soul.

** Karma Yogi – one who performs actions in soul-awareness, free from the
result of the actions.

*** OM SHANTI ***

Lord Of Life

*** OM Shanti ***

The Divine Father
*** Om Shanti ***

This poem is about seeing Divinity as the *Father of the soul*.
Remembering that I, the soul am completely independent
from the life I live.

When we remember this independence, we understand there is
a space of belonging for us beyond the physical,
material world.

This space is like a canopy of protection over the soul and
offers us safety and security. The canopy helps us develop
our awareness that *life is a gift*.

When falsehood takes root
Vice comes like mice
Steals inner strength, in a hole
Down here at length
Life becomes a strife
Like walking an edge of a knife
Hurry in the head, too much worry is fed
In comes the Lord of Life
Gives a gift, makes us shift and lift
Changes the ranges, the heads and hearts
Rebalances, for a start
Shows the true way to be a living art
To live truth, open the third eye
Say goodbye, to the world of earth
Come to the sweet silence home
Become clear, the spirit freer
From here live life
I take you back, so nothing lacks
Saves you from pain, shows you the correct lane
The Lord of Life
Takes the awareness to the original section

The journey from…

An awareness so selfish, one where arrows miss
To one lost in another's kiss, ego whisks
To awareness that does not recognise
The lies and cries, eyes only on one prize
Free from the upheaval, all the evil
Only a few, know it's nothing new
Be merciful to oneself, don't let it steal your wealth
Be gentle, the body is only rental
This is a wonder, the words struck like thunder !
Where this armour, perform perfect karma
Protected from the illusions
No more in confusions

*** OM SHANTI ***

Nourishment To Awaken

The Divine Mother
*** Om Shanti ***

This poem is about seeing Divinity as *a mother*.
The first nourishment a baby receives is their mother's milk
which awakens and strengthens the baby.

When we are *asleep*, we are unconscious of the *soul world*.
The term *awake* is about being aware of this soul world beyond
the physical. The more we *awaken*, the more we become
nourished by the energy from this world. This is achieved
through our regular efforts to connect to this
space during meditation.

This energetic nourishment, just like a mother's milk,
develops the strength of our *spiritual intellect*.

The Bestower of Fortune
In tune with every loon
Awakens the sleeping moon
A dormant fortune

Bestows a nourishment, seated at the front
First only regard, melts every lard
Love as an ocean
Brings an end to devotion

This Divine Mother says…

In this catchment, there will be attachments
Which is bad, as it makes you sad
Slowly going mad
Crying with whys, slowly dying in this lie
Sorrow is caused, through being entangled
Now it's time to take another angle
Now stay with detached affection, come into this section
See the bigger picture, frees you from the mixture

This energy nourishes become one who flourishes
Having this clear sight, on the infinite point of light
Will bring infinite delight
Opens the intellect, making things correct
So, continue to feed, from the seed

Feel lighter, become brighter
The intellect made fine, continue to refine
Always to remain kind
This the essence of the Divine
Wisdom is gained, when we are able to digest
To face every test, meet every moment at rest
Let the intellect be activated
Only in the Blissful One, be captivated
As an angel, safe guarded
Like the One, always regarded

*** OM SHANTI ***

Opening Of The Third Eye

Soul Awareness
*** Om Shanti ***

This poem is about the result of these first 2 relationships - *Divine Father* & *Divine Mother* with Divinity.

The third eye provides perception beyond ordinary sight; it is the driving seat in the centre of the forehead within our human body.

The third eye is our *soul awareness* which is an eternal living energy, our original and eternal identity which existed before we took on any material human identities and will exist after we pass away and let go of all these limited roles.

The dance of knowledge performed
Now taken out of the storm
The full history revealed
This removes wisdom's seal
Awakens our inner zeal
One becomes real
The story of the soul is told
Warms the heart from cold

In this liberation, defects mend and the soul cleansed
You are so elevated, so full of fortune
In tune with the moon
The plan, just to be a part of the highest clan
Stay within this meet, smile and greet

When karma in this drama is straight
No need to wait, it's all fate, it's all great
From the degrade, we get made, just fade
On this mountain don't be afraid

The old skin shed…Peaceful, as if in bed
A gentle hand, led, with crowns placed on the head
One of wisdom, purity and light
The other, strength, responsibility and might
This course brings double force
An image of success

Omens

OM Shanti

The Divine Astrologer
*** Om Shanti ***

A great deal of importance is put on astrology in the East.

When a child is born, their name is often chosen based on their astrological birth chart and ancient astrological science and art is often utilised to reveal all sorts of aspects, of a newly born life.

This poem explores this relationship of seeing Divinity as a *fortune-teller*. Our fortune is more than just wealth, it is also our health and happiness.

This Divine fortune-teller energy can play the role of lifting our burdens, dispelling negative omens, and bestowing us with lucky omens.

As the saying goes, *be and do good and good will always come back to you.*

Omens of luck, over time start to suck
Omens that only bring muck
From the top, there is the stop, then a big drop!

From 16 degrees full moon, to completely empty
In another tune, to the lowest point
It's all a descend, this the trend
Only then comes the fortune teller, the only feller
The only singer, the fortune bringer
Awakens with ankle bells, the ting tinger
Sees no country or nation, but asks for a donation
The donation of vice, I can make you nice
Have no desire, no tension of a tight wire
Give the lusts, the musts
They only make you rust
Anger so hot, inner wisdom rots
Breaks you with shots

Remember the body is a tool
Please, keep it cool
Give this donation, then the omens that suck
Will return back to luck
Kill the artificial frills, these omens only fill
From the fall, now grow tall
Check the self for thorns
Don't let it make you mourn or hot with scorn
Develop the power of silence
Still…Refine and then mill
My little chappy, let me make you happy !
Beautiful you will be, belong to One but for all to see
This wisdom is the fragrance
The musk, like white ivory tusks
When clean all is seen, eyes lean
When clear all will hear, with an open ear
This is the stance, to claim this inheritance

Intoxications

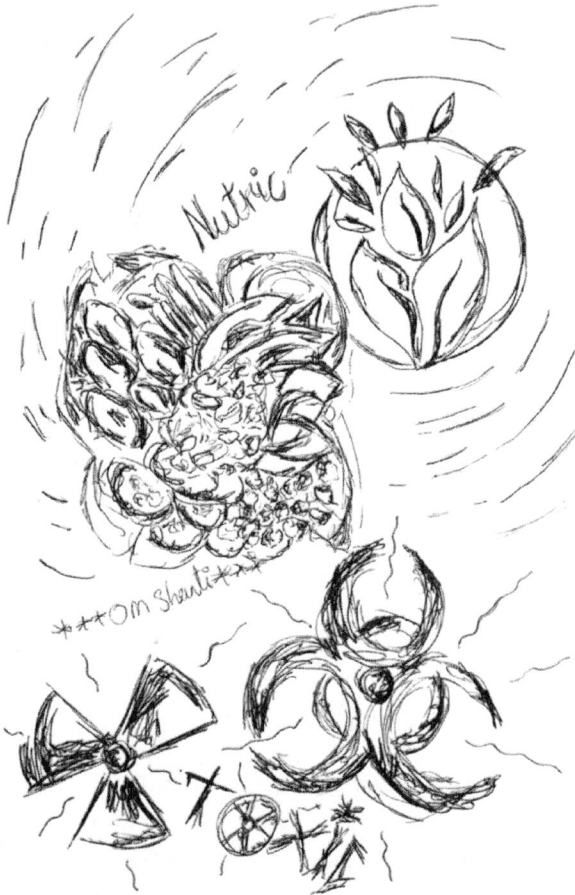

Nutric or Toxic
*** Om Shanti ***

This poem highlights the difference between
worldly intoxication and *spiritual intoxication.*

Worldly intoxication feeds the ego, and we start to feel superior
to others; this can become toxic to the mind as it creates an
unnecessary hierarchy.

Spiritual intoxication feeds the higher-self, and we start to
develop an appreciation of; *who I am*, and *what I have at
any given time.*

This is nutric to the mind, as it creates lightness which flows
with whatever is happening in our current times, free from
attachment.

Appreciation is key to maintaining a constant level
of happiness.

There are two types of intoxications
One of nation limited and in sound
One of creation unlimited and unbound

The one of nation creates an arrogance of health and wealth

However constant happiness is elusive
In personal relationships, exclusive
Following the chiefs of these old beliefs
Creates limited achievements
Leave one in bereavement
When change comes
A toxic intoxication

The one of creation is unending
I, the soul beyond any hole
Belong to the Divine Mother and Father
We are brothers and sisters
A divine family, correct this energy

The inheritance is a happy journey through life
Filled with peace, power and positivity

However, take time to be underground with no sound
Evolve, old problems dissolve
Fill the apron of these jewels, make them your tools
Allows us to become a perfect actor
One becomes a benefactor
Travels the Earth, increase everyone's worth

Surrender the mind and body
To give this donation, frees you from nations
To stay naturally in good health
Wealth and constant happiness

*** OM SHANTI ***

Time Travellers

The Illness & The Cure
*** Om Shanti ***

This poem highlights the differences in the levels of our consciousness; one level is limited with a *materialistic awareness* and the other level is unlimited with an expansive *soul awareness*.

Materialistic awareness can be seen like an illness which can be overcome with the medicine of soul awareness, which naturally cures by supporting a peaceful state of mind.

A traveller experiences all, the rise and the fall
Once a master, mind and body under cast
High on this mast

As we travel, a materialistic awareness causes a stall
To a downfall
Now ceased in this oldest disease, the root of all fleas
Changes the will, one becomes ill
Following this ark leads to just dark
Anger begins a cough
Trapped in different sounds
Attachment's war
The neck becoming sore
Locked in the world
Blocked the air flow of the nose
Changes the pose, heavy with burden
Hunchbacked for certain
The body shakes
A headache, weakens the state

The cure to this cold is the awareness of the soul
Unlimited is this role, plays only the part
Knows how to be a true art
Stable in the Purifier's meet
Remains cool and sweet
Feet never touching the ground
Not even a sound
With every toe, simply lets go

This is the position
Brings respect to all opposition
Just rise, one only flies in the mind
Brings out the light of the sunrise

An Honest Heart

*** OM SHANTI ***

The Divine Doctor
*** Om Shanti ***

This poem is about seeing Divinity as our healer. If we have an illness, we need to visit a doctor to obtain the advice and medicine needed to heal.

However, sometimes even when we are ill, we say, *I am fine* and suffer on as the ego stops us from acknowledging the illness.

The ego makes us dishonest at times, but the right support needed to overcome the illness can be sought from *The Divine Doctor.*

In order to remain close
To the One that knows the most
At the root, come from a place of truth
Be honest, he will be beyond, never astonished
The ocean of love, frees you of the fudge
Not yet the judge

This healer says…

All those mistakes, now stop and awake
All those crimes, for now have mercy, give it time
However, remain careful not to get caught up in a lull
Start to keep the record
Make this accord

If ego is to conceal, then the deal is too much feel
Also, an inner seal, the intellect becomes locked
Inner securities blocked
You will start to tilt, full of guilt

Self-esteem goes lower
The intellect's sharpness even slower
The cure not taken, insecure within shaken
Then there is fear, this closes the ear
If you suppress, this fills you with stress
Which turns to distress
Finally, the stall with a big fall

To be honest is to be humble, simply acknowledge
Then I can give you the right knowledge
From being ill, gain strength with this inner will
The Eternal Surgeon
Gives the injection that dissolves old rejections

Take this medicine, look within
The medicine is to return home
Makes you clean and clear
Keep my company for sure
The soul becomes pure

Detach the prong down there, not so long will it stay fair
Come above, you too can be an ocean of love
Experience silence so sweet
Lovely in this meet
Show disinterest, it will help you stay at rest
While facing every test

Know that from this sin, you have already won
Have this intoxication, while seeing all of creation
Then the face will reveal
The Divine Ones deal

Burner & Absorber

*** Om Shanti ***

The Laundry Man
*** Om Shanti ***

If thinking of our past suffering brings pain in our present life, then this is a sign that an emotional stain remains. The first step is to put a full stop to past suffering by burning it with the heat created by the washing machine when washing clothes.

We need to learn to forgive and forget and change our feelings towards this past suffering, so that it no longer has any control over our present-day emotional state.

However, the detergent must be very strong, and the washing cycle needs to be long enough to remove the stains.

Seeing the Divine as *The Laundry Man* will allow us to forgive and forget, put a full stop to the past and bring peace into our present.

When one's story is written, if soul awareness is shot
In the body we begin to blot, each test creates a mess
The punishment of canes, leaves many stains
Mistakes are made and the intoxication breaks
In the head creating many wasteful laps
Ends up hurting the heart
Lost the true art
To regain our sane...
See only The Purifier, sit in his glowing fire
Burn the past, no more does that last
Bring peace to the crier
Now the alloy that's mixed
Which performs tricks, removed, fixed
This is the cure to become pure
Put an end to the childish games
Surrounded by this One Flame
However, the stains take longer
This medicine is stronger
If you want to be a star, you have to remove the scars
Turn to the One Orb, He will absorb the blot
All that messy snot, no more your lot
Removes the pains and any stains
He will erase and change the case
Brings a smile to the face
Now, have mercy perform charity
Keep the stage sweet, always in this meet
Make others sweet, show the way to this seat

The highest business is...

To remind all to stay kind
Show this path to the blind, for all to find
Give this pure wish, it won't miss
An image of blessing, always flying with wings
This is a form, so true
Develops a power of truth

*** OM SHANTI ***

Holi Sprinkles Of Happiness

The Divine Lovers & Beloved
*** Om Shanti ***

This poem was written during the popular Indian festival of *Holi*, also known as the festival of love and colours. It happens in spring and celebrates the end of winter and the blossoming of love and life in nature, springtime.

It's a day of fun, play and laughter where people meet each other and spray each other with water and colours.

The spiritual message of this festival is to let go of the past, forgive, and repair broken relationships and to elevate our state of being (to become holy). So, that the goodness (light) within us can triumph over evil (dark).

The Beloved comes, free from any wrong
Sings a sweet song, enables all to belong
To belong is to burn the past
No more does that last
Let go of the old casts
Remove each wrinkle
With the spray of the colourful sprinkles

The sprinkles of being:

Elevated soul, diamond from coal
Child of the Supreme, as white and light as stream
Knowledge-full, the history in the intellect's pool
Finally, a true art
Plays a hero's part with the One
That makes all smart
On an elevated stage
A holy mage

The face pure and royal
The forehead's light emerges
Sight only on this delight
Wear this costume of light, a true fashion
Shows all compassion
In each actor's totality
See only the Beloved's specialty
Eat this instant fruit
You are so cute

Flowers In Bloom

The Divine Gardner
*** Om Shanti ***

This poem is about using Divinity to maintain order in our garden - *our mind is the garden*, and the intellect is the gardener.

A gardener's task is to maintain order in the garden, so it is not overrun with weeds (waste thoughts), hurtful thorns (self-sabotaging thoughts), or invasive fungus (cyclic thought patterns that invade our psyche).

Once a garden is in harmony, we can grow flowers which spread fragrance (pure and positive thoughts that strengthen the mind and spread a peaceful influence into our environment).

Love...Takes us above
Love so unending, untamed
Enable us to surrender to the flame
Earn a true income through remembrance of zero
Enables one to become a hero

Hero of health and wealth
Peace and prosperity, full of serenity
The old world renounced, take a big bounce
To the home of peace, feed this feast
The flute of wisdom played
From the fade, we are made

An intellect that's blocked
Maybe even shocked, made to unlock
However, be cautious, a thought of vice
Creates ice, then the keys will freeze, seize
Back to a lock, inner wisdom's block
A return to shock

Stop the indulge, as it makes the mind bulge
Then will come the habit of dirt
Where you will be hurt

Be flowers in bloom, loom
From a seed, never a wasteful weed
Your business is to churn, this will allow you to earn
Take full stock, the intellect remains unlocked
Spread this fragrance

Come into silence, as easy as sound
The heart lovingly pounds
The mission, to be an image that grants a vision
Be a master of all authority

The Greatness Of An Observer

*** OM SHANTI ***

The Silent Witness
*** Om Shanti ***

Discernment is the power of clear intellect, that inner voice of truth that guides our choices. If we quickly make closed-minded judgements, this will cloud our ability to discern.

The benefit of being an *impartial observer* is that we are beyond external influences. Allowing us to make clear and decisive judgements that have everyone's best interest at heart, so that we can serve others without any ulterior motives or ambitions.

A true sever is an elevated observer
Holds a court with every thought
Before spoken, takes token for every word
Free of the attraction, while performing every action
This is the way of the royals
Protected from being spoiled
Stage so stable, linked to One
This subtle cable

An easy fountain, beyond, on this mountain
A boundary that protects
From the effects, from a world gone sour
Stay in this lift, as it gives a special gift
To earn a good salary, see the world
As if it's an art gallery
This creates inner space, frees you from any race
Become strong and stable, like a mace
This is the measure that maintains inner pleasure

Always check...

Thoughts not caught in any storms
Aimless in its roam
Words take care, remember to keep them fair
Actions speak louder, keep them noble and prouder
This will improve your mood
Free from the simulation of situation
An end to pushing creation

This inner machinery improves the scenery
Constant stability comes
Through being absorbed in love
Like a dove, to the One above
Sing his song, simply belong
Joint, to this one point
Point to point

*** OM SHANTI ***

Pure As A Lotus - The Floating Flower

** * OM shanti * **

The Divine Teacher
*** Om Shanti ***

This poem is about seeing Divinity as our teacher. A teacher informs, educates, and instructs us to study well and pass our subjects. The main subject is to maintain *soul-awareness* and be like a lotus flower so that we can remain *above and beyond* the daily life challenges that we may face.

If one's own directions of desire are followed
Ego takes root, covered in soot
Arrogance pierces like a lance
No more is there a stable stance
One becomes trapped in a name and form
Like being stuck in the muddy silt
One begins to wilt, maybe bitten by guilt

This begins the endless roaming and romping
The mind, just storming and chomping
These wasteful laps, creates a sap that slaps
Lost sight of the true map
Wisdom's brunch not taken
Illusions' punch, left in delusions
Now, to become free of this confusion
Sit with my tuition
Be a diamond, valuable
One remains malleable
Makes one charitable

To remain clean is to enjoy every scene
On this world stage, while turning every page
To be a lotus flower
Always afloat, like a boat
Free from any minds bloat
The dirty water can take every quarter
So, remain in a form of light
Above
In a world of gentle might

Filled with this inner treasure, there is no measure
Put an end to the chase
Brings a sparkle on the face
Seen in the eyes, the forehead, only purity fed
This is the plan, to belong to this elevated clan
A true server

*** OM SHANTI ***

The Power Of Silence

*** OM shanti ***

The Divine Alchemist
*** Om Shanti ***

Alchemy is a process of changing something that has low value to something with a greater value (changing iron into gold).

This is just like our intellect that can be like iron, heavy brittle and set in its ways or like gold, which is light, flexible and malleable.

Spending time in silence, in divine company, is a magical process that allows us to drop the weakness that we may have acquired along our journeys of life. A transformation occurs on a molecular and chemical level in the brain when we are silent - our neurological pathways are rewired.

Seeing the Divine as an Alchemist helps us to develop our strength to move forward with calm and clarity on our life journey.

In a world of falsehood, most are stood in ego's hood
Unaware of our true value, ends up being unkind
In every task, evil spirits harass

The Divine Alchemist says...

Bring the mind to me, from unable to see
I make you free, bring peace to the mind
In silence...Stay kind, be stable in this stance
In unlimited love, absorbed, life's challenges, solved
Past sins, absolved, past weaknesses, dissolved

There is the ire of one fire, where alloy mixes
On a pyre of lust, traps and tricks
Then there is the gentle glow
Another fire, one that fixes, unmixes
Removes rust of old, turn into real gold
Pyre of yog (yoga)

If you get trapped, in a name or form
Sapped is the inheritance claim
Whatever you do, it's entirely all up to you
Live from truth, belong to the roots
An image of support speaks truth
Brings the age of truth

The eyes become jewels, that cools even the fools
Reveals the journey home and the story of each soul
This is the chance
To take beyond at a glance

Inheritance From Grandparents

The Divine Grandparent
*** Om Shanti ***

In an old Indian custom, an inheritance was passed from the grandparent to the grandchild, a legacy which skipped a generation. Seeing the Divine as our grandparent allows us to know we are guided and protected by generations past.

The Father so grand, unique is his land
Comes in the night
Brings peace to the fight
Changes us into light
Moments of delight !

From the mind numbing
So subtle is his coming
At the essence
Feel…His presence

The Grandfather says...

The only family plan, now is to take you to a new land
A land of liberation, frees you from each nation
A life of liberation, the wonder of all creation
Gives a place to belong

Teaches wise lessons, in every session
Merciful energy of the eyes, transforms the whys ?
Brings peace to the cries
Honesty and clarity, no lies

Changes the household of old
Shapes and moulds, transformed into real gold
Reveals secret stories, untold
Sits on an immortal throne, the perfect tone

Gives all a chance
To dance and claim an inheritance
From the start
To the moment he departs
It's all a beautiful art

*** OM SHANTI ***

Protectors Of The Holi Fire

The Divine Groom/Bride
*** Om Shanti ***

In Indian tradition during weddings, the bride and groom are seated in front of a fire. This fire ceremony is a vital part of starting a successful marriage, as fire is regarded as the purifier and the sustainer of life, bringing light, warmth and energy.

Sitting in front of a fire is a moment of surrender to one another in marriage and surrender to the Divine.

The fires symbolises the removal of all impurities and all that should be left is pure undiluted love, energy and life.

In a world gone blind, humans become unkind
The land become stark, like stumbling in the dark
From a land, incorporeal, but very real
A spark is ignited !

Begins a fire
This warm glow transforms the form
From a worthless shell, that left a bad smell
To as strong as a mace, one of the diamond race
Taken to a land free from storms

This importance recognised
Into this fire, sacrifice all the vice, put it in as fuel
Bring the mind into a state of yule
Bit by bit, the flames rise higher, tames all desires
When the heart becomes clean
The eyes sparkle a divine grace
Seen is the face's sheen
Able to cope with all the mope
The mind's elevated hopes
Always fulfilled
Seated on the heart throne
The stage capable, unshakable
Immovable and constant
Inspires others to attain sovereignty
Come into this sector
This fire's living protector

Cooperate, before it's too late
Your state may degrade
Learn to aid or the fortune fades
This fire is imperishable
As time moves on
All will enter, this fires centre
All will be gone
A world turns pure

*** OM SHANTI ***

The Company Of Truth

The Boatman & True Guide
*** Om Shanti ***

The intellect can be seen as a *boat on a journey*. When we travel alone, there may be some anxiety as we are responsible for sorting out all the details of our travels. If we are traveling with company the responsibility is shared and we feel more at ease.

However, this is only true if the company we keep is good - bad company could make us feel more anxious and even make us not want to take the trip.

This poem is about viewing the Divine as an experienced boatman who guides us on our journey. We don't need to take too much responsibility and we remain carefree and focused on the experiences along the way while our guide navigates us.

The company we keep
Can make us leap or fall really deep
Spiritual strength can clap or end up being sapped
Take us to the highest town or become a clown
Even drown

If the company is unsuited
There is an influence, strength is looted
Weakness arises, like spies changes the eyes
The actions performed become like storms
The boat struggles to stay afloat
There are needs to wear a coat*
Making excuses, lazy in a lull
Creates holes in the hull
Leakage, starts to seek, ego creeps in
Strengths seeps
If company is only in sound
Found at the bottom of the ocean
Drowned

To stay afloat, choose to remove the coat*
Take refuge, it's nothing huge, this One salvages
To stay afloat and protect the boat
Keep the company of three truths

The Father says...

Sit on my lap, from the sap
I reveal the true map, restarts the inner clap
Safe and protected

* Coat – projected self-image

The Teacher says...

Have an interest, to be the best
This study, puts you at rest
A status of royals, frees you of the mortal coil
Lamps alight by pouring this oil

The True Guide says...

Observe this order, hold this cord
Changes you into a lord
Check, ego does not take root
It will loot, leave you moot
Stay free of this rasp of illusions' grasp

This company makes one great, creates fate
Standing at these highest gates
The boat goes across

Now interact with tact, true acts of charity
Like fairies, delivering sweet berries
In this company of the truth
All will salute

The Benevolent One & His Partners

The Divine Boss/Business Partner
*** Om Shanti ***

Seeing the Divine as our *boss* allows us to take directions so that our time and energy are used in a worthwhile way and not wasted. Sometimes we need to be directed so that we can benefit ourselves and others to earn a good salary (in our spiritual bank account of positive karma/actions).

When we are wealthy enough, we can then become a *business partner* and encourage others around us to use their time and energy in a productive way too.

Little mistakes are made, causes a loss
When we forget who is boss
These little slips, causes many trips
From soul to body, the intellect becomes shoddy
The actions go wrong, simple things take too long
Slowly going ugly, covering in algae
On a pyre of lust, blazing in this impure fire
The poison of vice strikes a burning desire

The Benevolent One says...

Now it's time to break away
Come live the correct way
All that gloss, simply causes a 100% loss
Now, come up above, floss
Leave the ego, inspire
Take this benefit, it will fit, bring 100% profit
From this event, you also reinvent
Become benevolent

The occupation is to serve
Follow this natural curve
Enables you to be a seer, be creative and clear
Keeps the intellect loving, stay in this lift
Just uplift give this natural gift

However, be aware the battlefield
Remember to keep up your shield !
Incognito is this war
Careful not to become sore
Incognito is the shield that you wield
The one of 3 dots, protects each spot
Finish the sickness, all the incognito weakness

The essence of benevolent is to live, to give
A gift that uplifts

*** OM SHANTI ***

Directions Of The Creator

The Supreme Commander
*** Om Shanti ***

In an army, a *good soldier* is he/she who follows orders from their superiors even if they have a difference of opinion with the superior.

Every successful military unit has a clear chain of command and rests upon the fundamentals of discipline and obedience.

Seeing the Divine as our *commanding officer* will draw our attention to remove any spiritual carelessness and laziness that we may have acquired along our journey.

This commander may be strong and forceful but also nurtures us with love and comradery so that we can be the best soldier in our own life.

The enemy of ego, roams free
Unseen by sight
Could make one fall from a great height
The way to see and be free from this enemy

As creation, is to be led
Removes the dictates of the head, also others spread
Follow the resident of the land of golden red

Look at only the Supreme Commander
Who beats clean, as time ticks on
If dirt is thick, one could fall sick
The candle wick, blows out
The highest clan, only one stand

So have the courage to follow this discipline
He makes us strong
Sing only his song
Nothing ever goes wrong

Become a master ocean of love and peace
Always above
All parts of this journey
Loved

Awakened

The Guardian Angel
*** Om Shanti ***

Seeing the Divine as our *guardian angel* allows us to understand
that we are constantly supported and protected in ways we
need to be as humans – mentally, emotionally, physically
and spiritually.

Mentally, the angel helps us to maintain a child-like curiosity,
humility and a love for learning.

Emotionally, the angel helps us to not take issues too seriously
and maintain a sense of humour and lightness.

Physically, the angel helps us to keep the body active and
creative, such as singing, dancing, yoga and
eating well.

Spiritually, the angel helps us by creating space to breathe and
be in the awareness of the soul.

When we have aligned these four qualities in life, we can be
called an *awakened soul* - aware of our soulful state and using this
awareness to guide our way of being, seeing and doing.

In the sleep of ignorance, arrogance seeps in
A zest of many interests, the mind pulled in many tests
Fails to attain the highest crest
To awaken is to stop being shaken
To rise above with love
See arrogance's spies, now eyes only on one prize
Sing praise of the Purifier
The Peaceful One, the Blissful One
The Liberator and Guide, hold this hand
Through the waves and tides

From being like salty water, bossy and bitter
Come to my land, I will be the babysitter
It's time to remain simple
Make this property yours
Find true signs, grind in your own mind
The ocean churned within you, merged, now remerge
Have faith, interact with love and donate
This will create a stage that's awake

Faith In The Intellect

Faith Enables Victory
*** Om Shanti ***

The poem is about the quality of having faith.
To become victorious over the internal battles that we
experience, faith in *the self* is as essential as is faith in the Divine.

This enables us to have faith in the benevolent force of the
universe as there is always something to learn
in the trials we face.

Everything is done with the intellect
The acquiring of defects and the stage of becoming perfect
In the early morning hours
Shower and develop the intellect power
If waste is fed the intellect becomes dead
This boat can stay sound and pound along or end up
At the bottom of the ocean
Drowned

Have faith as big as a whale, this repairs the sail
Stay in the company of the truth

Stay free of lust's sword, that breaks the accord
Stops you from being a lord
From dishonesty, duality
Become centred on one singularity
True acts of charity

To keep the relationship close
Always stay in honesty's post
Detect falsehoods threats, eject this sect
This is to pass with all respect

The play is now coming to an end
It's time to transcend
Learn to take off the vest (bodily form)
Go into sweet disinterest
Enables you to attain
The highest crest

The Rosary Of Victory

Secrets On The Path Of Devotion
*** Om Shanti ***

This poem is about the qualifications of the *elevated souls* that have become *God-like*. In the devotion of some religions, they turn rosary beads while remembering the Divine. The number of beads can range from 8 to 108 - even up to 16108.

The symbolism is that each bead is a secret memorial of these *incognito elevated souls*. They have attained this by overcoming their internal battles and life challenges.

These souls are worthy of worship, like the Divine.

Awareness of looking only outwards
When the donation of this is made
End the darkness of jade
Learning how to fade
To a world free from sound
Become worthy
The value of the unlimited within pounds
The full knowledge within revealed
Opens this inner seal

Fully knowing...

The soul, jump out of the physical hole
The highest Father, rather to be his helper
The worlds of three, peace, love and mercy
The dimension of time truly
Understand this paradigm

Brings the experiences of virtue
Enable one to stand tall in this high tower
This is to be a child of the Supreme
Light and white like steam
One becomes totally free

Effort is to remain loyal
Practice being out of the mortal coil
Light within with this oil
Allows you to attain a status of royal
One that is wise and worthy of praise and prize

In a rosary threaded, a memorial created
Remembered, on every devotee's lips
While turning each tip
Worthy of worship

The Divine One & The Lords Of Divinity

°Om Shanti°

Signs Of A Divine Master
*** Om Shanti ***

This poem is about the result of being obedient and faithful to the Divine and the attainments of Trinetri, Trikaldarshi and Triloklinath.

Step into the Ocean, always in gentle motion
Waves that change the slaves, now it's time to behave
You are a lord, it's time to put down the sword

Let the third eye open, climb this rope
Wash with soap, have these elevated hopes
(Trinetri - Opening of the third eye)

This unlocks, inner wisdoms block
One become freer, able to discern, the seer unlocked
A knower of the history, unwind this mystery
(Trikaldarshi - A knower of the beginning, middle and end)

One is able to transform the form
From the gross, everyone knows the most
To wings of light, in a subtle land, bright mercy and might
To just a point like a star
From a peaceful land far, far
(Triloklinath - A master of 3 plains of existence)

Be a child with every smile, walk every mile
Enables one to draw strength, improves life's length
Take the injection to remove old infections and affections
From a thorn to a flower by imbibing this power
Then you can serve the spirit
Attain this merit, this divine credit
From a yard so grave, living in caves or soulless raves
To a world of delight, spread an angel's light

True spiritual pride, that can ride the tides
This is to be in the Ocean's eyes, to be a jewel
Always cool and under rule
The seeds of these deeds
Will always bear fruits and flowers
Spread fragrances and tastes
Such a beautiful state

*** OM SHANTI ***

The Light Of Purity Sparkles

*** om shanti ***

The Service Of A Pure Soul
*** Om Shanti ***

There are many forms of service, and this poem paints a
picture of the quality of service that is undertaken by a
pure soul, who not only undertakes good deeds but also shines
brightly through their facial features and their calm attitude
towards life. Their behaviour inspires us to be our best, as they
are examples of the *living arts*.

The sparkle on the face
Comes when we belonging to one race
A beauty to attain all types of fruity
A halo of might, a full circle, being bright
A tilak of light, a spark of a star, stood in brotherhood
A spiritual love in the eyes removes any remnants of ties
A sweet smile of the lips, gives wisdom tips
A face, belongs to one family the race
One Mother one Father

These lines of fortune, makes one fair, the quality of air
Free from any stain, washed away by the rain
Spreads a fragrance, sustains
One of being a child, light, easy, mild
One so real, full of zeal
On a seat, fed the right wheat
One of a lotus flower, impartial
Like a tortoise, able to stay true and straight
To tolerate

The Stage Of Retirement

Surrendered Living Arts
*** Om Shanti ***

When one comes into retirement, all worldly roles of a job and the concerns of earning an income come to an end.

We become carefree and when Divinity is awakened within us, it is like being in spiritual retirement.

In spiritual retirement we know that we have completed one part of our journey and that now we can transition into a surrendered life full of beauty and peace.

On a world stage, played through all ages
From a lord to the end of a sword
All within the record
Etched on the face can never be erased
From performing penance
To coming into the age of benevolence
Where each soul is re-kitted, benefited
Where we become a true mage
Part of the highest clan
Taken beyond with a wave of a magic fan

Taken into liberation, a true freedom from beliefs and nations
To a land above any quicksand
Alloy removed, made pure, take this natural cure
Free from the allure of a world unsure

Nothing to conceal, the truth will always be revealed
The Bestower of joy brings real toys for you to enjoy
The Purifier shaves burden away with a knife
Come into this
Stage of a retired life

The Divine
for undiluted love

Brahma Kumaris World Spiritual University
for inspiration

Paramjit Basra and Prashant Kakoday
for spiritual mentorship

Ash Patel, Shailen Popat and Marina Penkova
for support

Shobana Patel and the Soulful Group Imprint
for believing and publishing

Lisa Duffy
for proofreading support

The Reader
for your time and attention

Recommended reading: *Making Sense by Dr. Prashant Kakoday*

*** OM SHANTI ***

Bhavesh Ramji has a calm, warm and engaging personality. He is a practitioner and student of yoga, outdoor nature lover, artist, and poet. After passing through a series of tough life challenges, he experienced deep and profound love and compassion during his meditations. The poetry in this collection is an expression of those meditations. He regularly holds talks and seminars to share the wisdom behind his poems.

Oceans of Love: Part 1

A collection of poems and reflections which act as a guide in setting a solid foundation for developing a regular meditation practice.

Oceans of Love: Part 2

A collection of poems and reflections that take the reader on a journey of awakening and help develop a relationship with Divinity.

Oceans of Love: Part 3

A collection of poems and reflections that act as a treasure store of unlimited, invaluable hidden jewels of wisdom

Printed in Great Britain
by Amazon

21062325R00051